BOSTON COMMON PRESS
Brookline, Massachusetts

2000

Other titles in the *Cook's Illustrated*
How to Cook Series

HOW TO
MAKE QUICK
APPETIZERS

An illustrated step-by-step guide
to perfect party food.

THE COOK'S ILLUSTRATED LIBRARY

Illustrations by John Burgoyne

Copyright © 2000 by The Editors of *Cook's Illustrated*

Boston Common Press
17 Station Street
Brookline, Massachusetts 02445

ISBN 0-936184-43-4
Library of Congress Cataloging-in-Publication Data
The Editors of *Cook's Illustrated*
How to make quick appetizers: An illustrated step-by-step guide to perfect party food./
The Editors of *Cook's Illustrated*
1st ed.

Includes 41recipes and 29 illustrations
ISBN 0-936184-43-4 (hardback): $14.95
I. Cooking. I. Title
2000

Manufactured in the United States of America

Distributed by Boston Common Press, 17 Station Street, Brookline, MA 02445.

Cover and text design: Amy Klee
Recipe development: Kay Rentschler, Bridget Lancaster, and Julia Collin
Series editor: Jack Bishop

CONTENTS

introduction

W HEN WE'RE PREPARING AND SERVING
appetizers, that's usually not all we're
doing. We're also answering the front
door, pouring someone a drink, and
catching up with old friends who know their way to our
kitchen. Appetizers are, after all, party food. If we're the
hosts, we can bet that having lots of time to ourselves alone
in our kitchen is a very unlikely proposition.

The first challenge, then, when making appetizers is to
prepare food that doesn't keep us away from our guests for
very long. Most of the recipes in this book require twenty
minutes or less of hands-on preparation time, and we offer
ideas for doing as much ahead as possible.

Which appetizers we serve, and how many, will depend
on what sort of party we have. If it's a cocktail party with no
dinner following, we can serve lots of different foods,
including meats, without fear of overfilling our guests. But
if it's a short cocktail hour with dinner to follow, we'll be
careful to use appetizers to stimulate the appetite without

killing it. Once we get in the habit of building our appetizers around the party, choosing what and how much to serve becomes easy.

The difference between average appetizers and really good ones is usually found in the details. Crudités (raw vegetables) come out best when you know how they should be cut and whether or not they ought to be blanched before they're served. Spiced nuts, too often either overly sticky or overly oily, benefit from a very light glaze of liquid, sugar, and butter. We have found that wooden skewers used for Chicken Satay can easily be prevented from burning in the broiler with the use of aluminum foil. When the preparation is as simple as it is in these recipes, little things like this go a long way.

How to Make Quick Appetizers is the 21st book in the How to Cook Series published by *Cook's Illustrated,* a bimonthly publication on American home cooking. Turn to the beginning of the book for a complete list of titles in the series. To order other books, call us at (800) 611-0759 or visit us online at www.cooksillustrated.com. For a free trial copy of *Cook's,* call (800) 526-8442.

Christopher P. Kimball
Publisher and Editor
Cook's Illustrated

chapter one

APPETIZER BASICS

THE DICTIONARY DEFINES *APPETIZER* AS "a food or drink that stimulates the appetite." The French word *hors d'oeuvre* is translated as "apart from the work," and the Italian *antipasto* literally means "before the meal." Both are synonyms for *appetizer* and refer to the fact that these little fingers foods are eaten away from the dining table, often on the hoof. At a cocktail party, appetizers can be a meal unto themselves.

For this book, we have tested countless recipes for appetizer favorites from around the world, finally selecting the versions that taste best and require the least amount of work. In general, we have limited hands-on work to no more than 20 minutes for each recipe, plus baking and cooling times. Wherever possible we have provided do-ahead instructions to keep the cook out of the kitchen during the party.

The book is divided by the main ingredient in the appetizer (eggs, vegetables, meat, etc.). Within each chapter, we start with the recipes that are the easiest and quickest to make. Recipes at the end of each chapter tend to be a bit more complicated.

DECIDING HOW MANY APPETIZERS TO MAKE

The question we hear most often about appetizers concerns quantity. How many types of appetizers and how many pieces are required? The answer depends how long you plan to serve the appetizers and what follows. Some examples.

If you plan a short cocktail hour (let's say 45 minutes, while you wait for all of your guests to arrive) followed by a multicourse meal, you want to serve just one to two appetizers. (If you are expecting a large crowd, you might consider making three appetizers.) Plan on three or four pieces per person if you plan on one hour or less for cocktails. For more than one hour, make at least two appetizers and plan on four to six pieces per person.

A true cocktail party (with no dinner to follow) requires more types of appetizer and more pieces. In many cases, guests drink for several hours and some may even make a meal out of the appetizers. In this case, you want to serve at least five or six appetizers and should plan on at least 10 to 12 pieces per person.

Dips can be used to supplement the above recommendations, or, for a simple appetizer, you can serve a single dip and some crudités (raw vegetables) and skip the individual pieces.

Take into account how heavy and filling the appetizers you have chosen are. Guests are likely to be satisfied by two or three pieces of rolled beef but might want four or five large shrimp with cocktail sauce.

CHOOSING SPECIFIC APPETIZERS

The other area that perplexes many cooks is choosing particular appetizers. There are no hard-and-fast rules, but these guidelines should help.

Keep the season in mind, serving lighter foods in summer and heavier fare in winter.

Figure out where you plan to serve appetizers. If guests will be seated on sofas and can hold forks, knives, and plates, then almost anything will work. If guests will be gathering on foot, limit your selection to true finger foods and dips.

If you are serving dinner, plan the meal first and then use foods not already represented in the appetizers. For example, if your menu calls for steak, potatoes, and asparagus as the main course, you would not want to want to serve any of these foods as appetizers.

If serving more than one or two appetizers, choose appetizers that go well together. It's fine to have one rich appetizer with cheese, but don't serve three cheese appetizers. At cocktail parties, you will probably want a mix of hot and cold (or room temperature) appetizers.

For a shorter cocktail hour before dinner, you many want to stick with cold appetizers, which don't require any last-minute preparation. If you want to serve a hot appetizer, consider gathering guests in the kitchen so you don't have to slave away in solitude.

chapter two

DIPS AND SALSAS

IPS AND SALSAS ARE THE MOST BASIC party food. Put out a bowl of tomato salsa and chips or some creamy spinach dip and vegetables and most people will be satisfied. Cooks generally focus on the dip and don't give the accompaniments much thought. Chips are a given, but flatbreads and crackers work equally well. As for vegetables, we find that platters of raw broccoli and cauliflower are often inedible.

In our testing, we found the preparation of vegetables for crudités to be essential. There are two key elements: how the vegetable is sliced and whether or not it should be blanched (cooked briefly in salted boiling water) to make the texture more palatable and to improve its flavor.

The information that follows details the findings of our testing. When deciding which vegetables to use together for crudités, consider these factors: First and foremost, use what's in season and looks good at the market. Second, choose a variety of colors. A platter consisting entirely of green vegetables is not as attractive as a platter of green, white, yellow, orange, and red vegetables. Last, consider the texture of the vegetables. Crunchy, hard carrots work well with crisp, juicy bell peppers and soft cherry tomatoes.

Each of the preparations listed below yields about three cups of vegetables. Plan on serving 12 cups of vegetables with any of the dip recipes that follow. This translates to an average of four vegetables for a crudités platter to accompany a single dip.

ASPARAGUS: Snap tough ends from 12 ounces asparagus. Blanch in boiling salted water until bright green, 20 to 30 seconds. Drain, shock in ice water, drain again, and pat dry.

BROCCOLI: Cut florets from 1 small bunch (about 1 pound) into bite-sized pieces. Blanch in boiling salted water until bright green, about 1 minute. Drain, shock in ice water, drain again, and pat dry.

13

CARROTS: Blanch ¾ pound baby carrots in boiling salted water until bright orange, about 15 seconds. Drain, shock in ice water, drain again, and pat dry.

CAULIFLOWER: Cut florets from ½ medium head (about 1 pound) into bite-sized pieces. Blanch in boiling salted water until slightly tender, about 1 minute. Drain, shock in ice water, drain again, and pat dry.

CELERY: Trim ends from 4 medium stalks (about ½ pound). Cut stalks in half lengthwise, then crosswise into 3-inch lengths.

GREEN BEANS: Trim ends from 8 ounces thin green beans. Blanch in boiling salted water until bright green, 15 to 20 seconds. Drain, shock in ice water, drain again, and pat dry.

PEPPERS: Stem and seed 3 small red, yellow, or orange bell peppers. Cut into strips about 3 inches long and ¾ inch wide.

SUGAR SNAP PEAS: Remove ends and strings from 8 ounces sugar snap peas. Blanch in boiling salted water until bright green, about 15 seconds. Drain, shock in ice water, drain again, and pat dry.

TOMATOES: Stem 1 pound cherry tomatoes.

Classic Red Table Salsa

makes about 5 cups

➤ **N O T E :** *Our favorite Mexican-style salsa is perfect with tortilla chips. To reduce the heat in the salsa, seed the chile.*

3	large, very ripe tomatoes (about 2 pounds), cored and diced small
½	cup tomato juice
1	small jalapeño or other fresh chile, stemmed and minced
1	medium red onion, diced small
1	medium garlic clove, minced
½	cup chopped fresh cilantro leaves
½	cup lime juice
	Salt

I N S T R U C T I O N S :

Mix all ingredients, including salt to taste, in medium bowl. Cover and refrigerate to meld flavors, at least 1 hour and up to 5 days.

Chunky Guacamole
makes 2½ to 3 cups

➤ **NOTE:** *To prevent discoloration, prepare the minced ingredients first so they are ready to mix with the avocados as soon as they are cut. Ripe avocados are essential here. To test for ripeness, try to flick the small stem off the end of the avocado. If it comes off easily and you can see green underneath it, the avocado is ripe.*

3	medium, ripe avocados (preferably the pebbly skinned Haas)
2	tablespoons minced onion
1	medium garlic clove, minced
1	small jalapeño chile, stemmed and minced
¼	cup minced fresh cilantro leaves
¼	teaspoon salt
½	teaspoon ground cumin (optional)
2	tablespoons lime juice

▦ INSTRUCTIONS:

1. Halve one avocado, remove pit, and scoop flesh into medium bowl. Mash flesh lightly with onion, garlic, chile, cilantro, salt, and cumin (if using) with fork until just combined.

2. Halve and pit remaining two avocados. Following figures 1 and 2 (page 17), cut flesh into ½-inch cubes. Add cubes to bowl with mashed avocado mixture.

3. Sprinkle lime juice over diced avocado and mix entire contents of bowl lightly with fork until combined but still chunky. Adjust seasonings and serve. (Can be covered with plastic wrap, pressed directly onto surface of mixture, and refrigerated up to 1 day. Return guacamole to room temperature, removing plastic wrap at last moment, before serving.)

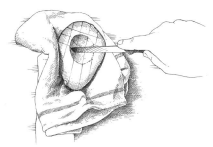

Figure 1.
Use a dish towel to hold avocado half steady. Make ½-inch crosshatch incisions in the flesh with a paring knife, cutting down to but not through skin.

Figure 2.
Separate diced flesh from skin using a spoon inserted between the skin and the flesh, gently scooping out avocado cubes.

Clam Dip with Bacon and Scallions
makes about 2 cups

➤ **NOTE:** *Regular or light sour cream and mayonnaise can be used in this dip and the one that follows. We found that lighter versions yield a slightly less creamy dip but are surprisingly good.*

4	strips (4 ounces) bacon, cut into ¼-inch pieces
¾	cup sour cream (regular or light)
¾	cup mayonnaise (regular or light)
1	teaspoon lemon juice
1	teaspoon Worcestershire sauce
2	cans (6½ ounces each) minced clams, drained
2	medium scallions, sliced thin
	Salt and ground black pepper
	Cayenne pepper

INSTRUCTIONS:

1. Fry bacon in small skillet over medium heat until crisp, 6 to 8 minutes. Transfer bacon with slotted spoon to plate lined with paper towel; let cool.

2. Whisk together sour cream, mayonnaise, lemon juice, and Worcestershire sauce in serving bowl. Stir in clams, scallions, and bacon. Season to taste with salt, pepper, and cayenne. Cover and chill until flavors meld, at least 1 hour and up to 2 days.

Green Goddess Dip
makes about 1³/₄ cups

➤ NOTE: *Mayonnaise adds body to this dip, while sour cream brings some needed tang and brightness.*

³/₄   cup sour cream (regular or light)
³/₄   cup mayonnaise (regular or light)
 2   medium garlic cloves, chopped
¼   cup fresh parsley leaves
 2   teaspoons chopped fresh tarragon leaves
 1   tablespoon lemon juice
 2   anchovy fillets, minced
¼   cup minced fresh chives
     Salt and ground black pepper

INSTRUCTIONS:

1. Combine sour cream, mayonnaise, garlic, parsley, tarragon, lemon juice, and anchovies in food processor and process until smooth and creamy, scraping down sides of bowl once or twice.

2. Transfer mixture to serving bowl and stir in chives. Season to taste with salt and pepper. Cover and chill until flavors meld, at least 1 hour and up to 2 days.

Hummus
makes about 2¹/₂ cups

➤ **NOTE:** *This Middle Eastern chickpea dip/spread flavored with tahini (sesame paste) is delicious with pita bread or pita chips as well as vegetables.*

1	can (19 ounces) chickpeas, drained and rinsed
1	large garlic clove, minced
6	tablespoons extra-virgin olive oil
¼	cup tahini
¼	cup lemon juice
¼	cup water
¾	teaspoon salt
	Pinch ground cayenne pepper
	Pinch ground paprika

⁞⁞ INSTRUCTIONS:

1. Combine chickpeas, garlic, 4 tablespoons oil, and tahini in food processor and process until smooth, scraping sides of bowl as necessary, about 30 seconds. Add lemon juice, water, salt, and cayenne and process again until smooth, an additional 10 seconds. Transfer hummus to serving bowl, cover, and chill until flavors meld, at least 1 hour and up to 24 hours.

2. To serve, use back of soup spoon to make a trough in hummus. Pour remaining 2 tablespoons oil into trough. Sprinkle with paprika and serve immediately.

Bagna Cauda
makes about 1½ cups

➤ NOTE: *Bagna cauda is a traditional hot anchovy dip hailing from the Piedmont region of Italy. It must be kept warm, so use a fondue pot or double boiler for serving. If you like your bagna cauda spicy, try the optional red pepper flakes. Serve with vegetables and bread.*

- 1 cup extra-virgin olive oil
- 5 tablespoons unsalted butter
- 3 medium garlic cloves, finely minced
- ½ teaspoon hot red pepper flakes (optional)
- 1 can (2 ounces) anchovy fillets, rinsed and drained
  Salt

INSTRUCTIONS:

1. Heat oil and butter in small, heavy-bottomed saucepan over medium-low heat until butter is melted and just begins to foam, about 3 minutes.

2. Add garlic and red pepper flakes (if using), and cook until garlic is fragrant but not colored, about 30 seconds. Add anchovy fillets and cook, stirring and mashing fillets with a wooden spoon until they become a paste. Season sparingly with salt to taste and serve, keeping mixture warm.

chapter three

CHEESE APPETIZERS

BUY CHEESE FROM A SOURCE YOU TRUST. Cheeses are fragile, and stores that don't handle them properly should be avoided. Always ask to taste a bit of any cheese before buying it. Cheese should not appear cracked, dried out, or—except for blue cheese—moldy. Buy small portions, no more than you will use in a week or so.

Once purchased, cheeses should be wrapped well. We find that wrapping cheese in layers of parchment (on the inside) and foil is best, followed closely by placing the cheese in a plastic bag and squeezing out all the air before sealing. While cheese should be stored in the refrigerator, always let cheeses come to room temperature before serving. The flavor and texture of most cheeses is improved at room temperature.

When serving several cheeses together, select a variety based on texture (soft, hard, crumbly), flavor (mild, sharp, pungent), and milk types (cow, sheep, goat).

Dates Stuffed with Parmesan
makes 16 pieces

➤ NOTE: *Use high-quality dates (such as Medjools) and only the finest Parmigiano–Reggiano in this appetizer.*

16   **large pitted dates**
1   **piece (3 ounces) Parmesan cheese**
16   **walnut halves, toasted**

INSTRUCTIONS:

1. Slit dates lengthwise with paring knife.

2. Following figures 3 and 4 (page 24), cut cheese into thin shards about one inch long. Place a piece of cheese and one walnut half in each date and close date around cheese to seal. Place dates on serving platter. (Dates can be wrapped in plastic and kept at room temperature for several hours.)

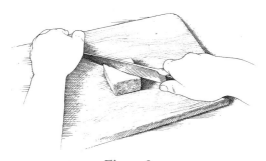

Figure 3.
Use a chef's knife to remove the rind from a square block of
Parmesan cheese. Cut the trimmed block in half on the diagonal.

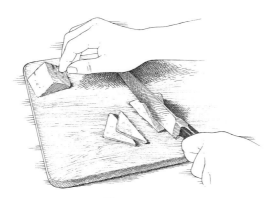

Figure 4.
Lay each half on its cut side and slice the cheese into thin
triangles, about $1/16$-inch wide. These thin shards should be
about the size of a date.

Warm Figs with Goat Cheese and Honey
makes 16 pieces

➤ NOTE: *The figs should be baked very briefly, just long enough to soften the cheese and warm the figs.*

16	walnut halves (about ½ cup)
1	tablespoon brown sugar
⅛	teaspoon salt
⅛	teaspoon ground cinnamon
1½	ounces goat cheese (about 3 tablespoons)
8	fresh figs, halved lengthwise
2	tablespoons honey

INSTRUCTIONS:

1. Combine walnuts, brown sugar, salt, and cinnamon in small, heavy-bottomed skillet over medium-high heat until sugar melts and coats nuts evenly, about 3 minutes. Remove nuts from pan, separating them from each other. Cool.

2. Adjust oven rack to middle position and heat oven to 500 degrees. Spoon heaping ½ teaspoon goat cheese onto each fig half and place on parchment-lined, rimmed baking sheet. Bake figs for 4 minutes. Transfer warm figs to serving platter.

3. Place a candied walnut half on each fig half and drizzle honey over figs. Serve immediately.

Marinated Goat Cheese
serves 4

➤ **NOTE**: *The garlic should be broken down into a fine puree for this recipe. After mincing, sprinkle the garlic with salt, mash the garlic-salt mixture with the side of a chef's knife, and then continue to mince until the garlic forms a smooth puree. Serve with bread or crackers.*

1	log (8 ounces) goat cheese
¼	cup extra-virgin olive oil
¾	teaspoon chopped fresh thyme leaves
¾	teaspoon minced fresh chives
¼	teaspoon minced fresh rosemary leaves
1	small garlic clove, minced and then worked into a puree with ⅛ teaspoon salt
	Ground black pepper

INSTRUCTIONS:

1. Following figure 5 (page 27), use a piece of dental floss to cut cheese crosswise into slices ⅓ inch thick.

2. Whisk together oil, thyme, chives, rosemary, garlic-salt puree, and pepper to taste in small bowl.

3. Pour oil mixture over cheese. Serve immediately or cover and refrigerate for up to 1 day.

Figure 5.
A knife quickly becomes covered with goat cheese, making it
difficult to cut clean, neat slices. A piece of dental floss is much
easier to use. Slide an 18-inch piece of floss under the cheese.
Cross the ends of the floss above the cheese and then pull the floss
through the cheese to make slices at ⅓-inch intervals.

Grilled Mozzarella and Sun-Dried Tomato Skewers
makes 24 skewers

➤ **NOTE**: *Use dried, loose tomatoes, not those packed in oil, for this recipe.*

48	large sun-dried tomatoes (about 3 ounces)
1	pound fresh mozzarella, cut into 1-inch cubes (you should have about 48 pieces)
3	tablespoons extra-virgin olive oil
1½	teaspoons salt
	Ground black pepper
48	small basil leaves

INSTRUCTIONS:

1. Adjust oven rack so that it is about 6 inches from broiler and heat broiler.

2. Combine ¾ cup water and tomatoes in medium microwave-proof bowl. Microwave for 30 seconds. Cover and let stand until tomatoes soften, about 5 minutes. Drain and blot dry on paper towels.

3. Meanwhile, toss mozzarella with oil, salt, and pepper to taste in medium bowl. Using 24 short bamboo or wooden skewers, thread a piece of mozzarella, basil leaf, and tomato

28

(in that order) onto each skewer; repeat with second piece of mozzarella, basil leaf, and tomato. Brush skewers with any oil remaining in bowl.

4. Line bottom of broiler pan bottom with foil and coat broiler pan rack with cooking spray. Place 12 skewers on broiler pan rack. Broil skewers, turning once, until cheese begins to melt, about 2 minutes. Remove from oven and let rest for 30 seconds. Pick up each skewer, twirling any melted cheese around the skewer (see figure 6, below), and serve immediately. Repeat with remaining skewers.

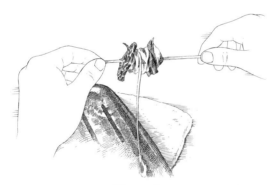

Figure 6.
The cheese melts slightly under the broiler. Once the skewers have cooled for about 30 seconds, pick up each skewer and spin it gently in your fingers to wrap any strings of melted cheese back around the skewers.

Honey-Baked Brie
Wrapped in Phyllo
serves 8

➤ NOTE: *A small wheel of brie can be wrapped in phyllo to form an extralarge beggar's purse. Serve the warm brie with a very sharp knife and spread it on crackers. The white, chalky mold that covers a wheel of brie can give off an ammonia-like odor when heated, especially if the cheese has been wrapped in packaging for some time and been unable to breathe. Remove the mold to prevent this problem. For this recipe, thaw a 1-pound box of phyllo (which has about 20 sheets) in the refrigerator overnight. Let the boxed phyllo come to room temperature on the counter for 2 hours.*

- 10   sheets frozen phyllo dough (about 8 ounces), thawed and brought to room temperature
- 1   wheel of brie (about 2 pounds, 6 inches in diameter)
- 5   tablespoons unsalted butter, melted
- 3   tablespoons honey

▦ INSTRUCTIONS:

1. Heat oven to 425 degrees. Remove phyllo from box and place on kitchen cloth that's just barely damp. Cover with another barely damp cloth and then a dry cloth to prevent phyllo from drying out.

2. Scrape white, chalky layer of mold off cheese rind, leaving remaining rind intact (see figure 7, page 31). Working

with one phyllo sheet at a time, brush about 1¼ teaspoons melted butter lightly over sheet and arrange according to figures 8 and 9 (page 32).

3. Place trimmed brie in center of phyllo layers. Use back of spoon to spread honey over top of brie. Following figure 10 (page 33), lift edges of phyllo to enclose cheese, gathering excess on top. Brush surface with remaining tablespoon of butter and place on parchment-lined, rimmed baking sheet.

4. Cover top of phyllo with piece of foil (see figure 11, page 33) and bake for 15 minutes. Remove foil and continue baking until phyllo is golden brown, about 5 minutes. Transfer brie to platter and serve immediately.

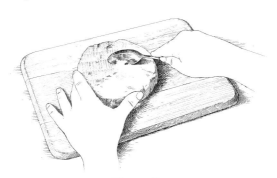

Figure 7.
Using a soup spoon, scrape the white, chalky layer of mold off the rind, leaving the remaining rind intact.

Figure 8.
Lay one sheet of phyllo on the counter and brush lightly with
butter. Lay a second sheet perpendicular to the first sheet
and brush with butter.

Figure 9.
Crisscross two more sheets of phyllo on top of the first two sheets,
buttering each as directed. Repeat the process with another four
sheets of phyllo, laying them perpendicular to each other. Lay the
final two sheets at right angles to each other on top of the pile.

Figure 10.
Once the cheese has been placed in the center of the phyllo, lift the
edges of the phyllo sheets up and over the cheese to enclose it.
Gather the excess phyllo on top and pinch together to form
a beggar's purse.

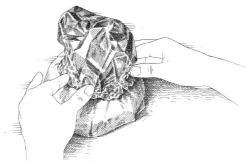

Figure 11.
Crimp the edges of a 5-inch square of foil. Carefully place the foil
over the pinched top of the phyllo to keep it from burning
in the oven.

chapter four

VEGETABLE
APPETIZERS

EGETABLES MAKE EXCELLENT APPETIZERS because they are generally light and refreshing. They are appropriate before a heavy meal, especially one that contains a lot of meat and/or cheese.

Vegetable appetizers can also be used to set the tone for a seasonal meal. It makes good sense to start a spring meal with fresh grown asparagus and a summer supper with marinated zucchini. Starchier vegetables, such as potatoes, are best for winter meals or cocktail parties where you want guests to feel more full.

Marinated Black and Green Olives
makes about 3 cups

NOTE: *These olives will keep in the refrigerator for at least a month and are perfect for impromptu entertaining. Ouzo is a sweet, licorice-flavored Greek spirit. You can substitute sambuca.*

8	ounces large, brine-cured green olives with pits
8	ounces large, brine-cured black olives with pits
5	large garlic cloves, crushed
3	large shallots, thinly sliced
1	teaspoon grated orange zest
1	teaspoon minced fresh thyme leaves
1	teaspoon hot red pepper flakes
½	cup ouzo
¼	cup extra-virgin olive oil
¾	teaspoon salt
	Pinch cayenne pepper

INSTRUCTIONS:

1. Drain olives into colander and rinse them well under cold running water. Drain olives well.

2. Combine remaining ingredients in glass or plastic bowl. Add olives and toss to combine. Cover and refrigerate for at least 12 hours. Remove from refrigerator at least 30 minutes before serving.

35

Prosciutto-Wrapped Roasted Asparagus

makes about 20 pieces

➤ NOTE: *Make sure you have the same number of asparagus spears and pieces of prosciutto (count them once they have been cut into 3-inch lengths). The number should be around 20.*

1	pound thin asparagus spears, tough ends snapped off
1	teaspoon extra-virgin olive oil
	Salt and ground black pepper
1	teaspoon balsamic vinegar
3	tablespoons grated Parmesan cheese
3	ounces thinly sliced prosciutto, cut crosswise into 3-inch pieces

INSTRUCTIONS:

1. Adjust oven rack to highest position and heat broiler. Toss asparagus with oil on rimmed baking sheet. Sprinkle with salt and pepper to taste. Broil, shaking pan halfway through to turn asparagus, until lightly browned, about 5 minutes.

2. Sprinkle asparagus with vinegar and cheese. Cool slightly. Wrap a piece of prosciutto around bottom half of each asparagus spear, making sure to leave the tip of the asparagus exposed. Arrange asparagus on platter and serve immediately.

Small Potatoes Stuffed with Bacon and Cheese

makes 16 pieces

➤ N O T E : *It's important to remove as much of the potato flesh as possible, leaving behind just a very thin layer attached to the skin.*

8	small red or white potatoes, about 2 ounces each
	Salt
4	slices bacon (about 4 ounces), finely chopped
1	small onion, minced
1	medium garlic clove, minced
2½	ounces cream cheese, softened
2	tablespoons minced chives
	Ground black pepper
1¼	ounces sharp cheddar, very thinly sliced

▪▪ I N S T R U C T I O N S :

1. Bring 6 cups water to boil in medium saucepan. Add potatoes and 2 tablespoons salt and boil, partially covered, until potatoes are tender, 20 to 25 minutes.

2. Meanwhile, fry bacon in small, heavy-bottomed skillet over medium-high heat until crisp, about 5 minutes. Use slotted spoon to transfer bacon to plate lined with paper towels and pour off all but 1 tablespoon bacon fat from skillet.

3. Add onion to remaining fat in skillet. Sauté over medium heat until golden, about 3½ minutes. Add garlic and cook for 30 seconds. Remove pan from heat.

4. When potatoes are done, drain and cool slightly. (It is important that the potato flesh be hot when processed with the other ingredients, so don't cool to much.) Following figure 12 (page 39), halve and hollow out potatoes, placing potato flesh in medium bowl along with bacon, onion mixture, cream cheese, chives, and salt and pepper to taste. Using electric mixer, beat mixture on medium speed until just combined, about 10 seconds.

5. Adjust oven rack so that it is 6 inches from broiler, and heat broiler. Following figure 13 (page 39), stuff potatoes and arrange in shallow 9-inch metal pie pan. Broil 10 minutes. Remove potatoes from broiler and top each half with slice of cheddar. Return potatoes to broiler and broil until cheese melts, about 5 seconds. Serve immediately.

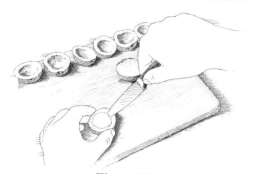

Figure 12.

*Cut the potatoes in half around the equator. Trim a very thin
slice from the end so each piece will sit flat on the counter. Use a
paring knife to trace a neat outline just inside the skin of the
potato. Use a small spoon to scrape out the flesh inside the circle,
leaving a thin band of flesh attached to the skin.*

Figure 13.

*Using a small spoon, stuff a small amount of cheese-flavored
potato mixture back into each potato half, mounding the filling
slightly over the top of the potato half.*

Roasted Mushroom Caps
Stuffed with Sausage
makes 24 pieces

➤ **N O T E :** *Prepare stuffing while mushrooms caps are roasting.*

24	large mushrooms, stems discarded and caps wiped clean
2	tablespoons olive oil
	Salt and ground black pepper
12	ounces bulk pork sausage
4	slices white bread, torn into large pieces
1	large shallot, coarsely chopped
1	large garlic clove, coarsely chopped
1	tablespoon mustard
2	teaspoons balsamic vinegar
2	tablespoons port wine
3	tablespoons grated Parmesan cheese
1	large egg, lightly beaten

I N S T R U C T I O N S :

1. Adjust oven rack to lowest position and heat oven to 450 degrees. Toss mushroom caps, oil, and salt and pepper to taste in medium bowl. Arrange caps, gill-side down, in single layer on large baking sheet. Roast until mushrooms have released some juice and are brown around edges, about 15 minutes. Remove pan from oven and turn caps over with metal spatula. Continue to roast until mushroom liquid has evaporated completely and mushroom caps are uniformly brown, 5 to 10 minutes longer.

2. Meanwhile, place sausage in medium skillet over medium-high heat and sauté until brown, about 5 minutes. Drain excess fat.

3. Place cooked sausage, bread, shallot, and garlic in food processor. Pulse until coarsely chopped, about 10 one-second pulses. Transfer filling to small mixing bowl and stir in remaining ingredients, including 1 teaspoon ground black pepper.

4. When mushrooms caps are uniformly brown, remove pan from oven and fill each mushroom with a heaping tablespoon of filling (or more depending on mushroom's size). Continue baking until filling is golden brown and hot throughout, about 15 minutes. Transfer to platter and serve immediately.

Corn Fritters
makes 30 small cakes

➤ **NOTE:** *These fritters are delicious on their own but are even better when topped with a dollop of sour cream and smoked salmon or chive-flavored sour cream and caviar.*

2	cups frozen corn kernels, partially thawed
1	large egg
3	tablespoons flour
3	tablespoons cornmeal
2	tablespoons heavy cream
1	large shallot, minced (about 3 tablespoons)
1¼	teaspoons salt
	Pinch cayenne pepper
¼	cup vegetable oil for frying, or more as needed

INSTRUCTIONS:

1. Combine all ingredients except oil in food processor and pulse until mixture forms thick batter, with some whole kernels and bits of corn still visible, about ten 1-second pulses. (The batter can be covered and refrigerated for several hours.)

2. Heat oil in 12-inch skillet over medium-high heat until it shimmers, about 2 minutes. Using a measuring teaspoon, drop silver-dollar-sized rounds of batter into oil (half the batter, or 15 fritters, should fit into the skillet at once). Fry until golden on one side, about 40 seconds. Using a thin metal spatula, turn fritters and fry until other side is golden, about 40 seconds more. Drain fritters on triple thickness of paper towels. Maintaining heat in skillet, repeat with remaining batter, adding more oil if necessary. Serve immediately.

Cocktail Potato Pancakes
makes 30 small cakes

➤ **NOTE:** *Serve these miniature potato cakes with a dollop of sour cream or apple sauce.*

2	pounds Yukon Gold or russet potatoes, peeled
1	medium yellow onion, peeled and cut into eighths
1	large egg
2	tablespoons minced fresh chives
3	tablespoons matzo meal
1½	teaspoons salt
	Ground black pepper
1	cup vegetable oil for frying

INSTRUCTIONS:

1. Grate potatoes in a food processor fitted with coarse shredding blade. Place half of potatoes in fine mesh sieve set over medium bowl and reserve. Fit processor with steel blade, add onion, and pulse with remaining potatoes until mixture looks coarsely chopped, about six 1-second pulses. Combine with potatoes in sieve and toss together, pressing to extract as much liquid as possible from potatoes into bowl beneath. Let potato liquid stand until starch settles to bottom, then pour off liquid, leaving starch in bowl. Beat

44

egg, potatoes, chives, matzo meal, and salt and pepper to taste into starch.

2. Heat half of oil in 12-inch skillet over medium-high heat until shimmering, about 3 minutes. Meanwhile, invert a rimmed baking sheet and cover with aluminum foil or parchment paper. Using a tablespoon measure, form half potato mixture into 15 cakes on back of baking sheet. Transfer cakes one by one to hot oil with thin metal spatula. Fry until golden brown on one side, about 3 minutes. (Use this time to form remaining cakes on back of baking sheet.) Turn with spatula and continue frying until golden brown on second side, about 3 minutes more. Drain pancakes on triple thickness of paper towels.

3. Pour oil from pan and wipe clean with paper towels. Add remaining ½ cup oil to pan and heat over medium-high heat until shimmering. Fry remaining pancakes as directed above. Serve immediately.

chapter five

MEAT AND CHICKEN APPETIZERS

MEAT APPETIZERS STRIKE US AS COCKTAIL party food. Most are substantial, so that if dinner is soon to follow, you should offer something light, like Prosciutto-Wrapped Melon, or small portions of sliced meats, such as prosciutto and salami, served with bread, olives, and cheese.

Most meat appetizers must be served hot. We suggest ways to prepare as much as possible in advance (sauces can generally be made and other ingredients can be prepared and often skewered), but meat appetizers usually involve some last-minute cooking.

Prosciutto-Wrapped Melon
makes 32 pieces

➤ **NOTE**: *To use a honeydew melon, cut one half into 16 crescents, then cut crescents in half crosswise. Reserve remaining melon for another use.*

> 1 **medium cantaloupe**
> ¼ **pound thinly sliced prosciutto, cut into 2 by 5-inch pieces**

INSTRUCTIONS:

1. Trim rind from melon, cut melon in half, and scoop out seeds with spoon. Cut each half into eight ½-inch-wide crescents. Cut each crescent in half crosswise.

2. Following figure 14 (below), wrap one piece of prosciutto around each melon slice. Serve immediately or cover and refrigerate for up to 2 hours.

Figure 14.
Take a piece of prosciutto and carefully wrap it around the thicker end of each melon slice.

Kielbasa Wrapped in Puff Pastry
makes 14 to 16 pieces

➤ NOTE: *The key to success with this recipe is rendering some of the sausage fat, which keeps the puff pastry from becoming soggy. Pastries can be made ahead and frozen for up to two weeks or made ahead and refrigerated for several hours before baking.*

1	pound kielbasa
1	sheet (10 by 9½ inches) commercial puff pastry, still partially frozen, cut in half
2	large eggs, lightly beaten
¼	cup grainy mustard

▪▪ INSTRUCTIONS:

1. Heat oven to 425 degrees. Cut kielbasa in half crosswise and pierce several times with fork. Roll it in 2 layers of paper towel and microwave on high for 1 minute to release some of the fat; set aside to cool.

2. Meanwhile, place one half of puff pastry between two layers of parchment paper and use a rolling pin to stretch pastry into rectangle that measures about 10 by 7 inches. Brush pastry edges with beaten egg. Following figure 15 (page 49), roll pastry around sausage. Brush exterior with egg. Place seam-side down on parchment-lined, rimmed baking sheet. Repeat with second piece of puff pastry and kielbasa and place on same baking sheet. Put baking sheet in freezer for 10 minutes.

3. Bake until deep golden brown, 20 to 25 minutes. Remove from oven and allow to rest for 5 minutes. Slice diagonally into ½-inch slices. Arrange slices on platter and serve immediately with a small bowl of mustard.

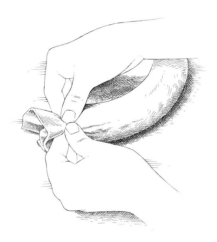

Figure 15.
Place a piece of kielbasa on the longer edge of the puff pastry.
Roll the kielbasa in the pastry and then pinch
in the ends to seal.

49

Indian-Style Meatballs with Apricot Sauce
makes 36 meatballs

➤ **N O T E :** *We found that freezing the meatballs briefly before frying helps them hold their shape.*

Indian-Spiced Meatballs

1	pound ground lamb
1½	teaspoons salt
1	teaspoon ground cumin
1	teaspoon ground coriander
¼	teaspoon garam masala
⅛	teaspoon cayenne pepper
2	tablespoons minced fresh cilantro leaves
2	tablespoons yogurt
1	slice white bread, chopped (about 5 tablespoons)
2	tablespoons vegetable oil

Apricot Sauce

1	cup apricot preserves
¼	cup port wine
1	tablespoon balsamic vinegar
⅛	teaspoon ground cinnamon
¼	teaspoon hot red pepper flakes
1	tablespoon fresh minced mint leaves
	Salt and ground black pepper

INSTRUCTIONS:

1. Mix all ingredients for meatballs except oil in large bowl. Shape into 36 meatballs, each about 1 inch in diameter. Place on parchment-lined baking sheet and freeze for 5 minutes.

2. Meanwhile, combine apricot preserves, port, vinegar, cinnamon, and red pepper flakes in small saucepan over medium-high heat. Bring to a simmer and remove from heat. Stir in mint and salt and pepper to taste. Transfer sauce to serving bowl and cover to keep warm.

3. Heat heavy-bottomed, 12-inch skillet over high heat until very hot, about 4 minutes. Add oil to pan and swirl to coat bottom. Lay half of meatballs in pan and cook, turning occasionally, until well browned, 5 to 6 minutes. Transfer to serving platter. Repeat with remaining meatballs. Place bowl with apricot sauce on platter and serve immediately, with toothpicks.

Asian-Style Beef and Scallion Rolls
makes 35 to 40 pieces

➤ NOTE: *Freezing the meat makes it easier to slice. Rolls can be assembled up to four hours in advance and browned to order.*

1⅓	pounds flank steak, trimmed of excess fat and frozen for 20 minutes
10	scallions, green part only, cut into 2-inch lengths (see figure 16, page 53)
2	tablespoons vegetable oil
2	medium garlic cloves, minced
1	tablespoon minced fresh gingerroot
1	teaspoon hot red pepper flakes
¼	cup tamari sauce
3	tablespoons mirin or sherry

▋ INSTRUCTIONS:

1. Cut flank steak in half lengthwise. Following figure 17 (page 54), slice each half crosswise on the bias as thinly as possible. You should have about forty 2 by 3-inch pieces. Place meat slices between 2 sheets of parchment paper and pound to a uniform thickness, about ⅛ inch. Pieces will measure 3 by 5 inches. Roll each piece of beef up tightly around two or three pieces of scallion (see figure 18, page 54).

2. Heat heavy-bottomed large skillet over medium-high heat until hot, about 4 minutes. Add oil and heat briefly until it shimmers. Lay 20 beef rolls in skillet, seam-side down, and sauté, without moving, until browned, about 1 minute. Using tongs, turn rolls to brown on all sides, about 2 minutes more. Remove rolls from pan and set aside on plate to rest. With pan still hot, repeat with remaining beef rolls, transferring them to same plate to rest when done.

3. Add garlic, ginger, and red pepper flakes to empty pan; sauté until fragrant, scraping up any browned bits from bottom of pan, about 10 seconds. Add tamari, mirin, cooked beef rolls, and any accumulated juices on plate. Simmer to finish cooking beef, about 1 minute. Transfer beef to a serving platter and pour sauce into small serving bowl. Skewer beef rolls and place bowl with sauce on platter. Serve immediately.

Figure 16.
Use a pair of scissors to snip the scallion greens into 2-inch lengths. Make sure to separate the several green portions at the top of most scallions and snip each one. A single scallion will yield as many as ten 2-inch lengths of greens.

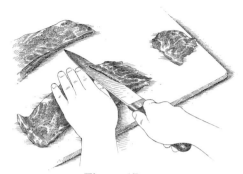

Figure 17.
Cut the flank steak in half lengthwise. Then slice each half crosswise as thinly as possible on the bias. You will be cutting against
the grain of the meat.

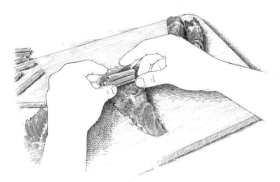

Figure 18.
Once the slices of meat have been pounded, place two or three
pieces of scallion over the meat and roll tightly, starting at a short
end, to seal. The meat is sticky enough to seal without skewers.

Seared Flank Steak with Horseradish Sauce

makes 40 pieces

➤ **NOTE:** *We strongly recommend using crème fraîche in this recipe. It has a firmer texture than sour cream (which can be watery in sauces like this) and better flavor.*

Flank Steak

1½	**pounds flank steak, trimmed of excess fat and patted dry with paper towels**
	Salt and ground black pepper
2	**tablespoons vegetable oil**

Horseradish Sauce

1	**cup crème fraîche or sour cream**
3	**tablespoons prepared horseradish**
1	**tablespoon lemon juice**
¼	**teaspoon sugar**
	Salt and ground black pepper

INSTRUCTIONS:

1. Heat heavy-bottomed, 12-inch skillet over high heat until very hot, about 4 minutes. While skillet is heating, season steak with salt and pepper to taste. Add oil to pan and swirl to coat bottom. Lay steak in pan and sauté, not moving it, until well browned, about 3½ minutes. Turn meat with

55

tongs; sauté until browned on second side, about 3½ minutes more. Transfer steak to plate and let rest for 10 minutes.

2. While steak rests, mix all ingredients for horseradish sauce, including salt and pepper to taste, in small serving bowl.

3. Following figure 17 (page 54), slice steak crosswise on the bias into slices ⅛ inch thick. Halve longer slices into 3-inch lengths. Roll up each slice tightly, skewer with toothpick, and transfer to serving platter. Place bowl with sauce on platter and serve immediately.

Chicken Satay with Spicy Peanut Sauce

makes 16 skewers

➤ **NOTE:** *Thai red curry paste is sold in many supermarkets. Look for it near the fish sauce and rice noodles. It has a complex, spicy flavor. An equal amount of hot red pepper flakes will provide the peanut sauce with adequate heat, but the sauce will lack the complex flavor provided by the curry paste.*

¼	cup low-sodium soy sauce
2	tablespoons vegetable oil
2	tablespoons Asian sesame oil
2	tablespoons honey
6	small garlic cloves, minced (about 2 tablespoons)
¼	cup minced fresh cilantro leaves
1	tablespoon minced fresh gingerroot
2	medium scallions, white and green part, sliced thin
4	boneless, skinless chicken breasts (about 4 ounces each)

Spicy Peanut Sauce

5	tablespoons creamy peanut butter
2	tablespoons lime juice
⅓	cup unsweetened coconut milk
1	tablespoon minced fresh gingerroot

    2   **medium garlic cloves, minced**

    1   **teaspoon Thai red curry paste or hot red pepper flakes**

    1   **teaspoon sugar**

■ **I N S T R U C T I O N S :**

1. Adjust oven rack to highest position and heat broiler. Whisk together soy sauce, vegetable oil, sesame oil, honey, garlic, cilantro, ginger, and scallions in large bowl. Cut chicken breasts on diagonal into 16 strips, each about 3 inches long and 1 inch wide. Add chicken to bowl and marinate, stirring occasionally, for 15 to 20 minutes.

2. While chicken marinates, place all ingredients for peanut sauce in blender or food processor and process until smooth. Scrape sauce into small serving bowl.

3. Thread each chicken piece lengthwise on its own short bamboo or wooden skewer. Place skewers on a broiler rack over foil-lined broiler pan bottom. Cover exposed ends of skewers with foil (see figure 19, page 59). Brush chicken with marinade remaining in bowl and broil until golden brown, about 2½ to 3 minutes, turning skewers half-way through. Place skewers on platter with bowl of peanut sauce. Serve immediately.

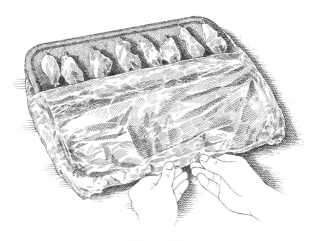

Figure 19.
To keep the exposed portions of the skewers from burning
(the portion people will use as a handle to hold the skewers),
cover the ends of the skewers (but not the chicken) with foil.

chapter six

SEAFOOD
APPETIZERS

EAFOOD MAKES A LIGHT, REFRESHING APPETIZER. The recipes that follow either start with smoked fish (salmon or trout) or call for cooking the seafood in some fashion.

Raw seafood, however, is often so simple to serve that you don't really need a recipe. Clams on the half shell are delicious on their own or with a dollop of cocktail sauce (see page 64). Choose either littlenecks or cherrystones (the latter are larger) for shucking. Oysters, which can be served like clams, are a bit more complicated to buy. There are five main species and hundreds of varieties, usually named for the places where the oysters are found. Buy oysters from a reputable source and taste several kinds to figure out whether you prefer crisp, briny Atlantic oysters from northern waters; softer, flabbier Atlantic oysters from the Gulf; fruity, sweet Pacific oysters; briny and metallic-tasting European or flat oysters; or briny but sweet Kumamotos.

Clams, oysters, and mussels can also be grilled just until they open (5 to 10 minutes depending on their size). Once the bivalves open, serve with lemon wedges, barbecue sauce, or a little hot sauce.

Smoked Salmon Mousse
makes about 1¹/₄ cups

➤ NOTE: *This tasty spread has multiple applications. It can be piped into hollowed-out cherry tomatoes (use a melon baller to remove the seeds), onto snow peas and endive leaves, or into little tart shells. Our favorite way to use this spread is as a canapé topping for squares of black bread.*

4	ounces sliced smoked salmon
1	large shallot, minced (about 3 tablespoons)
2	ounces cream cheese, softened
1	tablespoon lemon juice
¼	cup crème fraîche or sour cream
	Ground black pepper

⁚⁚ INSTRUCTIONS:

1. Place salmon and shallot in food processor and process until mixture is finely chopped, scraping down bowl as necessary, about 10 seconds. Add cream cheese and lemon juice and process again until mixture forms a ball, again scraping down bowl as necessary. Add crème fraîche and pulse just to incorporate, 5 seconds.

2. Turn mousse into bowl and season with pepper to taste. Use immediately or cover with plastic wrap and refrigerate up to 2 days.

⁚⁚ VARIATION:

Smoked Trout Mousse

Replace salmon with ½ pound smoked trout fillets (about 2 fillets), skinned and broken into pieces. Substitute lime juice for lemon juice. Increase crème fraîche to ⅓ cup. Add 2 tablespoons well-drained prepared horseradish with crème fraîche.

Broiled Shrimp Wrapped with Bacon
makes 24 pieces

➤ NOTE: *We found that blanching makes the bacon a bit less salty and is worth the extra couple of minutes of work.*

4	**slices bacon (about 4 ounces)**
24	**small shrimp (about 8 ounces), peeled**
1	**tablespoon balsamic vinegar**
	Salt and ground black pepper

▪▪ INSTRUCTIONS:

1. Stack bacon strips on top of each other and halve lengthwise; cut strips diagonally into thirds. Bring 1 quart of water to a boil in medium saucepan. Add bacon and blanch for 50 seconds. Drain bacon and lay flat on triple thickness of paper towels.

2. Adjust oven rack to highest position and heat broiler. Wrap one piece bacon around each shrimp and place on broiler rack, tucking ends of bacon under shrimp. Sprinkle shrimp with balsamic vinegar and salt and pepper to taste.

3. Broil until shrimp are pink and edges of bacon are brown, about 2 minutes, reversing direction of broiler pan after 1 minute. Transfer to a platter and serve immediately, with toothpicks.

Shrimp Cocktail
makes 16 to 20 pieces

➤ **NOTE:** *Cooking the shrimp in a quick shrimp stock made with the shells gives them a real flavor boost. If using smaller shrimp, decrease cooking time for shrimp by one to two minutes.*

Herb-Poached Shrimp

1	pound very large (16 to 20 per pound) shrimp, peeled, deveined, and rinsed, shells reserved
1	teaspoon salt
1	cup dry white wine
4	peppercorns
5	coriander seeds
½	bay leaf
5	sprigs fresh parsley
1	sprig fresh tarragon
1	teaspoon lemon juice

Cocktail Sauce

1	cup ketchup
2½	teaspoons prepared horseradish
¼	teaspoon salt
¼	teaspoon ground black pepper
1	teaspoon ancho or other mild chili powder
	Pinch cayenne pepper
1	tablespoon lemon juice

II I N S T R U C T I O N S :

1. Bring reserved shells, 3 cups water, and salt to boil in medium saucepan over medium-high heat; reduce heat to low, cover, and simmer until fragrant, about 20 minutes. Strain stock through sieve, pressing on shells to extract all liquid.

2. While stock is simmering, combine all ingredients for cocktail sauce in small bowl. Adjust seasonings. Cover and refrigerate sauce to blend flavors, at least 1 hour and up to several days.

3. Bring stock, wine, spices, herbs, and lemon juice to a boil in 3- or 4-quart saucepan over high heat; boil 2 minutes. Turn off heat and stir in shrimp; cover and let stand until firm and pink, 8 to 10 minutes. Drain shrimp, reserving stock for another use.

4. Plunge shrimp into ice water to stop cooking, then drain again. Refrigerate shrimp until well chilled, at least 1 hour and up to several hours. Serve chilled shrimp with cocktail sauce.

Cocktail Crab Cakes
makes 24 small cakes

➤ **N O T E :** *The amount of bread crumbs you add will depend on the juiciness of the crabmeat. Start with just 2 tablespoons. If the cakes won't hold together once you have added the egg, add more bread crumbs, one tablespoon at a time.*

Crab Cakes

1	pound jumbo lump crabmeat, picked over to remove cartilage and shell
4	scallions, green part only, minced (about ½ cup)
1	tablespoon chopped fresh parsley leaves
1½	teaspoons Old Bay seasoning
2 to 4	tablespoons fine dry bread crumbs
¼	cup mayonnaise
	Salt and ground white pepper
1	large egg
½	cup flour
6	tablespoons vegetable oil

Creamy Dipping Sauce

¼	cup mayonnaise
¼	cup sour cream
2	teaspoons minced chipotle chiles
1	small garlic clove, minced
2	teaspoons minced fresh cilantro leaves
1	teaspoon lime juice

6 6

▪▪ I N S T R U C T I O N S :

1. Gently mix crabmeat, scallions, parsley, Old Bay, 2 table-spoons bread crumbs, and mayonnaise in medium bowl, being careful not to break up crab lumps. Season with salt and white pepper to taste. Carefully fold in egg with rubber spatula until mixture just clings together. Add more crumbs if necessary.

2. Invert a rimmed baking sheet and cover with parchment paper. Using a generous tablespoon, form mixture into 24 cakes, each 1½ inches in diameter and ½ inch thick. Place each finished cake on baking sheet. Cover with plastic wrap and chill at least 30 minutes. (Can be refrigerated up to 24 hours.)

3. While cakes are chilling, combine all ingredients for sauce in small bowl. Cover and refrigerate to blend flavors, at least 30 minutes and up to 2 days.

4. Adjust oven rack to middle position and heat oven to 200 degrees. Line a baking sheet with double thickness of paper towels. Put flour on plate or in a pie tin. Lightly dredge half the crab cakes, knocking off excess.

5. Meanwhile, heat heavy-bottomed 12-inch skillet over medium-high heat for 4 minutes. Add 3 tablespoons oil and lay floured cakes gently in skillet; pan-fry until outside is crisp and brown, 1½ to 2 minutes. (Flour remaining cakes while first batch is browning.) Using a metal spatula, turn cakes. Sauté until second side is crisp and brown, 1½ to 2 minutes. Transfer finished cakes to baking sheet lined with paper towels and place sheet in oven.

6. Pour off fat from hot skillet and wipe clean with paper towels. Return skillet to heat, add remaining 3 tablespoons oil, and heat 1 minute. Add remaining cakes and pan-fry as above. Serve hot with dipping sauce.

Steamed Shrimp Wontons with Thai Dipping Sauce
makes 24 pieces

➤ NOTE: *You can make the shrimp filling one day ahead but should assemble the wontons as close to serving time as possible or the filling will weep. Look for wonton wrappers in the refrigerator case of your supermarket. The dipping sauce becomes more flavorful if prepared a day in advance.*

Shrimp Wontons

- ½ pound raw medium shrimp, peeled and deveined
- 1 teaspoon grated or finely minced fresh gingerroot
- 1 medium garlic clove, chopped
- 1 medium scallion, thinly sliced
- 2 teaspoons Asian chili paste
- 1 large egg white
- 24 square wonton wrappers

Thai Dipping Sauce

- ¼ cup rice wine vinegar
- 2 tablespoons fish sauce
- 1 tablespoon sugar
- 1 large garlic clove, thinly sliced
- ½ small carrot, peeled and coarsely grated
- ¼ teaspoon hot red pepper flakes

INSTRUCTIONS:

1. Place shrimp, ginger, garlic, scallion, chili paste, and egg white in food processor and process until well blended, about 1 minute. Transfer to small bowl and refrigerate until ready to use.

2. Mix all ingredients for sauce together in small bowl. Set aside for at least 10 minutes or up to 1 day for flavors to develop.

3. Follow figures 20–22 (page 71) to shape wontons. Spray a collapsible steamer basket with vegetable spray. Fill large Dutch oven or heavy-bottomed stockpot with enough water to reach bottom of basket. Bring to simmer over medium-low heat and lower basket into kettle. Arrange 12 wontons ½ inch apart in basket. Increase heat to high, cover, and steam until dumplings are cooked through, about 5 minutes. Remove wontons from steamer basket and repeat with remaining wontons. Serve with dipping sauce.

Figure 20.
Position a square wonton wrapper with one point facing you. Place 2 teaspoons of filling in the center. Fold the wrapper in half to form a triangle. Press to seal edges.

Figure 21.
Fold the long edge containing the filling over, leaving the top of the triangle exposed by about half an inch.

Figure 22.
Moisten the underside of the right point, then bring the two points together, right over left, to overlap, away from the tip of the triangle. Pinch the points together to seal the dumpling.

chapter seven

EGG APPETIZERS

WO KINDS OF EGG DISHES MAKE SENSE AS appetizers. Deviled eggs start with hard-boiled eggs that have been halved. The yolks are removed, enriched and seasoned, and then piped back into the empty whites. The key to perfect hard-boiled eggs is removing the pan from the heat as soon as the water comes to a boil and then letting the eggs steep, covered, in the hot water for exactly 10 minutes.

The other main type of egg appetizer is a fully cooked, flat omelet, which is called a *tortilla* in Spain or a *frittata* in Italy. These thick egg "cakes" can be sliced into wedges or cut into bite-sized squares. They can be served hot or at room temperature, making them ideal for entertaining.

Deviled Eggs
makes 8 pieces

➤ NOTE: *In some eggs, the yolks set very close to the bottom of the whites and it is difficult to remove the yolks and still keep the whites in tact as a serving vessel. For this reason, we boil five eggs, using the yolks from all five but discarding the white from one egg, figuring that one egg is likely to have this problem.*

You may double or triple this recipe as long as you use a pot large enough to hold the eggs in a single layer, covered by an inch of water. The eggs can be boiled one day in advance. After piping in the egg yolk mixture, however, they can be refrigerated for only up to two hours before serving.

5	large eggs
1	tablespoon mayonnaise
1	tablespoon unsalted butter, melted
1	teaspoon Dijon mustard
½	teaspoon rice wine vinegar
⅛	teaspoon Worcestershire sauce
⅛	teaspoon salt
⅛	teaspoon ground black pepper
	Dash Tabasco sauce
2	teaspoons minced fresh chives

▓ INSTRUCTIONS:

1. Place eggs in medium saucepan, cover with 1 inch water, and bring to a boil over high heat. Remove pan from heat, cover, and let stand for 10 minutes. Meanwhile, fill a

medium bowl with 1 quart cold water and 1 tray of ice cubes (or equivalent).

2. Transfer eggs to ice water bath with slotted spoon; let sit 5 minutes. Following figures 23 and 24 (page 75), peel eggs and then slice in half lengthwise. Remove yolks and place in small bowl. Place whites on platter, discarding two halves that look the worst, and set aside.

3. Mash yolks with fork until no large lumps remain. Add mayonnaise, butter, mustard, vinegar, Worcestershire sauce, salt, pepper, and Tabasco, and blend with wooden spoon until well mixed.

4. Fit pastry bag with medium star tip. Fill pastry bag with egg yolk mixture. Pipe yolk mixture into reserved egg halves, mounding filling slightly above egg halves (see figure 25, page 75). Sprinkle ¼ teaspoon chives over each egg half. Serve.

Figure 23.
Tap the egg all over
against the counter surface,
then roll it gently back
and forth a few times on
the counter to crack the
shell all over.

Figure 24.
Begin peeling from the
air pocket end (the wider
end) of the egg. The shell
should come off in spiral
strips attached to a thin
membrane.

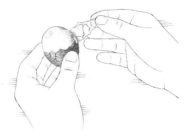

Figure 25.
A pastry bag fitted with a
star tip makes the most
attractive deviled eggs. If
you don't own a pastry
bag, spoon the yolk mix-
ture into a sealable plastic
bag. Snip a small piece
from one bottom corner of
the bag and then gently
squeeze the filling
through the hole into the
egg halves.

Spanish Omelet
makes 12 or more pieces

➤ **N O T E :** *This dish, called* tortilla española, *is a thick, golden brown cake of eggs, potatoes, and onions. Serve with some sliced Spanish ham (called* serrano*), a hunk of manchego cheese, and a bowl of olives to make a traditional tapas.*

3	tablespoons extra-virgin olive oil
1	large onion, halved and thinly sliced
2	small garlic cloves, minced
12	ounces red potatoes, thinly sliced
6	large eggs, lightly beaten
1	teaspoon minced fresh thyme leaves
	Salt and ground black pepper

I N S T R U C T I O N S :

1. Heat 2 tablespoons oil in 10-inch nonstick skillet over medium heat. Swirl skillet to distribute oil evenly over bottom and sides. Add onion; sauté until softened, 3 to 4 minutes. Add garlic, sauté until fragrant but not colored, about 1 minute. Transfer onion mixture to medium bowl and reserve.

2. Still over medium heat, add remaining tablespoon oil to skillet and swirl to distribute evenly. Add potatoes, toss to coat potatoes with oil, cover, and cook, stirring occasionally, until potatoes are tender, 13 to 15 minutes. Transfer potatoes to bowl with onions. Add eggs and thyme, stirring to coat well; season with salt and pepper to taste.

3. Add entire mixture back to skillet over medium heat. Stir lightly with fork until eggs start to set. Once bottom is firm, lift omelet edge so that uncooked egg runs underneath (see figure 26, below). Continue cooking about 40 seconds, then lift edge again, repeating process until egg on top is no longer runny, about 8 minutes.

4. Cover skillet with a large buttered plate and carefully flip the omelet out. Gently slide omelet back into pan, cooked side up, and cook until completely set and golden brown, about 4 to 5 minutes longer. Run spatula around skillet edge to loosen omelet; slide onto serving plate. Cut into thin wedges or 1-inch squares, season with salt and pepper to taste, and serve immediately or at room temperature.

Figure 26.

Once the bottom of the omelet or frittata is firm, use a thin spatula to lift the edge closest to you. Tilt the skillet slightly toward you so that uncooked egg runs underneath. Return the skillet to level position and swirl gently to distribute the uncooked egg.

Asparagus Frittata with Mint and Parmesan
makes 12 or more pieces

➤ NOTE: *An Italian frittata is similar to a Spanish omelet, but the texture is lighter and fluffier. Putting the frittata under the broiler (rather than flipping it) helps create this texture. Blanch the asparagus in salted water until crisp-tender, about 1½ to 2 minutes.*

2	tablespoons extra-virgin olive oil or unsalted butter
1	shallot, minced
1	tablespoon minced fresh mint leaves
2	tablespoons minced fresh parsley leaves
⅓	pound asparagus, tough ends snapped off and discarded; spears cut into 1-inch pieces and blanched until crisp-tender
5	tablespoons grated Parmesan cheese
¼	teaspoon salt
¼	teaspoon ground black pepper
6	large eggs, lightly beaten

⁑ INSTRUCTIONS:

1. Adjust oven rack to upper-middle position and heat oven to 350 degrees.

2. Heat oil or butter in 10-inch nonstick, ovenproof skillet

over medium heat. Swirl skillet to distribute evenly over pan bottom and sides. Add shallot and sauté until softened, 3 to 4 minutes. Stir in mint, parsley, and asparagus; toss asparagus to coat with oil. Spread in single layer.

3. Meanwhile, stir 3 tablespoons cheese, salt, and pepper into eggs. Pour mixture into skillet; stir lightly with fork until eggs start to set. Once bottom is firm, use thin spatula to lift frittata edge closest to you. Tilt skillet slightly toward you so that uncooked egg runs underneath (see figure 26, page 77). Continue cooking about 40 seconds, then lift edge again, repeating process until egg on top is no longer runny.

4. Sprinkle remaining 2 tablespoons cheese over frittata. Transfer skillet to oven; bake until frittata top is set and dry to touch, 2 to 4 minutes, making sure to remove frittata as soon as top is just set. Run spatula around skillet edge to loosen frittata; slide onto serving plate. Cut into thin wedges or 1-inch squares and serve immediately or at room temperature.

chapter eight

BREAD
AND PASTRY
APPETIZERS

THIS CHAPTER CONTAINS RECIPES FOR BRU-
schetta, quesadillas, biscuits, and phyllo
triangles. *Bruschetta* is an Italian appetizer
that starts with slices of broiled or grilled
country bread that are rubbed with garlic, brushed with
olive oil, and topped with everything from chopped tomatoes to olive paste. The *quesadilla* comes from Mexico and
is a hot "sandwich" made with two tortillas. This tortilla
sandwich is usually filled with cheese (and other ingredients) and cut into narrow wedges for serving.

Biscuits are an all-American favorite. For use as an appe-

8 0

tizer, they need to be cut quite small. In our recipe, we split and fill the biscuits with ham and cheese after they have been baked.

This chapter ends with a recipe for phyllo triangles. In our testing, we found that phyllo must be slowly brought to room temperature to prevent sticking or cracking. This means thawing phyllo (which is almost always purchased frozen) overnight in the refrigerator and then bringing it to room temperature in the box. To keep phyllo from cracking, keep sheets in a stack between two barely damp cloths until you need them.

Master Recipe

Bruschetta with Fresh Herbs

makes 16 small slices

➤ **NOTE:** *This is the simplest bruschetta, but delicious. The variations are slightly more complicated.*

5	tablespoons extra-virgin olive oil
1½	tablespoons minced fresh parsley leaves
1	tablespoon minced fresh thyme or oregano leaves
1	tablespoon minced fresh sage leaves
	Salt and ground black pepper
1	loaf country bread (about 12 by 5 inches), cut lengthwise in half and sliced crosswise into 1-inch-thick pieces (ends saved for another use)
1	large garlic clove, peeled

INSTRUCTIONS:

1. Adjust oven rack to highest position and heat broiler.

2. Mix oil, herbs, and salt and pepper to taste in small bowl. Set aside.

3. Place bread on large baking sheet; broil bread until golden brown on both sides. Place toast slices on large platter, rub garlic over tops, brush with herb oil, and serve immediately.

82

Bruschetta with Tomatoes and Basil

Combine 4 medium ripe tomatoes (about 1⅔ pounds), cored and cut into ½-inch dice, with ⅓ cup shredded fresh basil leaves and salt and pepper to taste in medium bowl and set aside.

Follow master recipe, reducing oil to 3 tablespoons and omitting parsley, thyme, and sage. Once toasts have been broiled, rubbed with garlic, and brushed with oil, use slotted spoon to divide tomato mixture among toast slices and serve immediately.

Bruschetta with Black Olive Paste

Process 3 tablespoons extra-virgin olive oil, 1½ cups pitted kalamata olives, 2 teaspoons fresh rosemary leaves, 2 tablespoons shredded fresh basil leaves, 1 tablespoon rinsed capers, and 4 rinsed anchovy fillets in food processor, scraping down sides with rubber spatula, until mixture is finely minced and forms a chunky paste, about 1 minute. Transfer to small bowl and set aside.

Follow master recipe, reducing oil to 3 tablespoons and omitting parsley, thyme, and sage. Once toasts have been broiled, rubbed with garlic, and brushed with oil, use a small spoon to spread olive paste lightly over toasts and serve immediately.

Avocado and Cheese Quesadilla
makes 8 pieces

➤ **NOTE:** *We find that an electric knife is the best tool for cutting a quesadilla into wedges. Serve as is or with a little Classic Red Table Salsa (page 15).*

2   soft, 8-inch flour tortillas

1   medium ripe Haas avocado, halved, pitted, flesh removed and coarsely chopped

½   small garlic clove, minced

2   tablespoons minced fresh cilantro leaves

1   teaspoon lime juice
     Salt and ground black pepper

3   thin slices red onion

2   ounces pepper Jack cheese, coarsely grated
     Nonstick cooking spray

INSTRUCTIONS:

1. Adjust oven rack to middle position and heat oven to 450 degrees. If tortillas are uneven in size, trim them with a scissors to match.

2. Combine avocado, garlic, cilantro, and lime juice in small bowl and mash coarsely with fork. Season with salt and pepper to taste. Spread mixture evenly over one tortilla, leaving ½-inch border around circumference free. Arrange onion slices over avocado and sprinkle with cheese, leaving ½-inch border. Place second tortilla over cheese and press slightly to position.

3. Heat 10-inch nonstick skillet over medium heat for 2 minutes. Coat top tortilla with vegetable spray and place quesadilla, greased side down, into pan. Cook until golden brown and crisp, about 2 minutes. Coat top tortilla with vegetable spray. Using a wide metal spatula, flip quesadilla in pan. Cook until second side is golden brown and crisp, about 2 minutes more.

4. Transfer quesadilla with metal spatula to small baking sheet and place in oven until hot throughout, about 3 minutes, flipping once halfway through. Cut into 8 wedges and serve immediately.

Cheddar Biscuits with Ham and Swiss

makes about 30 pieces

➤ **NOTE:** *These biscuits are best served at once, though they may be wrapped and refrigerated for a day, then reheated for a few minutes in a 350-degree oven. Assemble just before serving.*

Cheddar Biscuits

2	cups all-purpose flour, plus extra for work surface
1	tablespoon baking powder
¾	teaspoon salt
3	tablespoons chilled unsalted butter, cut into ¼-inch cubes
3	tablespoons chilled vegetable shortening
1	cup shredded cheddar cheese (about 4 ounces)
¾	cup cold milk
2	tablespoons unsalted butter, melted

Ham and Cheese Filling

5	tablespoons honey mustard
1	pound thinly sliced ham, cut into 3-inch lengths
½	pound thinly sliced Swiss cheese, cut into 1-inch pieces

⠿ INSTRUCTIONS:

1. Adjust rack to center position and heat oven to 450 degrees.

2. Pulse together flour, baking powder, and salt in food processor. Add chilled butter and shortening; process until mixture resembles dry oatmeal. Transfer to large bowl. Add cheese and toss lightly with rubber spatula or fork. Stir in milk until dry ingredients are just moistened. Let dough rest for 1 minute, then transfer to a well-floured work surface.

3. Pat dough into a rough 6 by 10-inch rectangle. Using a lightly floured 1½-inch biscuit cutter, stamp out dough rounds, cutting them close together. Dip cutter into flour before each new cut. Push scraps of dough together so that their edges join, and firmly pinch edges with fingertips to seal. Pat dough into small rectangle and cut more biscuits. (You should have about 30 altogether.) Place dough rounds 1½ inches apart on two ungreased baking sheets. (Baking sheets may be covered with plastic wrap and refrigerated up to 3 hours.)

4. Brush dough rounds with melted butter. Bake until biscuits are lightly browned, 8 to 10 minutes. Let cool slightly on wire rack until just warm. Split each biscuit in half. Arrange bottom halves on platter. Spread ½ teaspoon mustard on each biscuit half. Loosely arrange a slice of ham over mustard, then place a piece of cheese on top of ham. Set tops of biscuits in place and serve.

Phyllo Triangles
makes 24 pieces

➤ **NOTE:** *For this recipe, thaw a 1-pound box of phyllo (which has about 20 sheets) in the refrigerator overnight. Let the boxed phyllo come to room temperature on the counter for 2 hours. The triangles can be made several weeks in advance and frozen on a baking sheet. When ready to bake, take the triangles straight from the freezer and bake as directed, increasing the time by 10 or 15 minutes.*

Sausage and Cheese Filling

¼	pound ground sweet Italian sausage
¼	pound ground turkey or veal
1	large egg yolk
1	tablespoon bread crumbs
2	tablespoons grated Parmesan cheese
2	tablespoons grated provolone cheese
2	tablespoons ricotta cheese
1	medium garlic clove, chopped

Goat Cheese and Olive Filling

8	ounces goat cheese, at room temperature
8	black olives, pitted and chopped
2	tablespoons pine nuts, toasted and chopped
2	teaspoons grated lemon zest
1	teaspoon minced fresh thyme leaves
1	medium garlic clove, minced
	Pinch salt

| 16 | sheets frozen phyllo dough (about 13 ounces), thawed and brought to room temperature |
| ½ | pound (2 sticks) unsalted butter, melted |

■■ I N S T R U C T I O N S :

1. If making sausage and cheese filling, process all ingredients in food processor until well blended, about 1 minute. Transfer to small bowl and refrigerate until needed. If making goat cheese and olive filling, use rubber spatula to combine all ingredients in small bowl and refrigerate until needed. (Both fillings can be refrigerated up to 1 day.)

2. Remove phyllo from box and place on barely damp kitchen cloth. Cover with barely damp cloth and then a dry cloth to prevent phyllo from drying out.

3. Adjust oven racks to upper-middle and lower-middle positions and heat oven to 425 degrees. Following figures 27 through 29 (pages 90–91), assemble triangles. Place triangles seam-side down and about 1 inch apart on two parchment-lined baking sheets. Freeze for 10 minutes.

4. Brush each triangle top with 1 teaspoon of remaining butter. Bake until golden brown, for a total of 13 to 15 minutes, switching position of baking sheets halfway through cooking. Remove baking sheets from oven and cool triangles on sheets for 5 minutes. Serve immediately.

Figure 27.
Brush a phyllo sheet with 1½ teaspoons melted butter.
Place a second sheet of phyllo directly on top of the first sheet and
brush it with 1½ teaspoons of butter. Cut sheets lengthwise to
make three long doubled strips of phyllo, each about 4 inches
wide. Fold each strip in half lengthwise.

Figure 28.
Place 2 level teaspoons of filling on the corner of one strip and fold up the phyllo to form a right-angled triangle.

Figure 29.
Continue folding up and over, flag-folding style, until you reach the end of the strip. Repeat figures 28 and 29 with remaining two strips of phyllo. Once you have made three triangles, start over again with two new pieces of phyllo and repeat figures 27 through 29.

chapter nine

POPCORN
AND NUTS

PICED NUTS ARE A PARTY FAVORITE. MOST recipes calls for a heavy sugar syrup, which leaves the nuts very sticky. Another popular option is to sauté the nuts in butter, but we found that this method dulls the finish of the nuts and makes them taste oily. After testing some alternatives, we decided to coat the nuts in a light glaze made from very small amounts of liquid, sugar, and butter. This treatment leaves the nuts shiny and just tacky enough for a dry spice coating to stick perfectly, giving the nuts a beautiful appearance and excellent flavor.

Making flavored popcorn is even easier. Simply cook seasonings in a little melted butter to bring out their flavor and then toss with hot, fresh popcorn.

Cajun Popcorn
makes 3 quarts

➤ NOTE: *To pop the corn needed for this recipe, heat a wok over medium-high heat for 4 minutes, add 2 tablespoons vegetable oil, and ½ cup popcorn kernels. Cover, then cook, shaking constantly, until kernels stop popping, 2½ to 3 minutes.*

3	**tablespoons unsalted butter**
¾	**teaspoon Tabasco sauce**
1	**teaspoon hot red pepper flakes**
½	**teaspoon garlic powder**
¼	**teaspoon onion powder**
¼	**teaspoon dried thyme**
½	**teaspoon paprika**
½	**teaspoon salt**
⅛	**teaspoon ground black pepper**
3	**quarts plain freshly popped popcorn**

▪ INSTRUCTIONS:

1. Combine all ingredients except popcorn in small saucepan and cook over medium-low heat until butter has melted and mixture begins to foam, 2 to 3 minutes. Cover and set aside to keep warm.

2. Place hot popcorn in large bowl, drizzle with butter mixture, and toss until evenly coated. Serve warm or at room temperature.

93

Warm-Spiced Pecans with Rum Glaze
Makes about 2 cups

➤ **NOTE:** *Store spiced nuts in an airtight container for up to 5 days.*

> 2   **cups raw pecan halves (8 ounces)**

Warm Spice Mix

> 2   **tablespoons sugar**
> ¾   **teaspoon kosher salt**
> ½   **teaspoon ground cinnamon**
> ⅛   **teaspoon ground cloves**
> ⅛   **teaspoon ground allspice**

Rum Glaze

> 1   **tablespoon rum, preferably dark**
> 2   **teaspoons vanilla extract**
> 1   **teaspoon brown sugar**
> 1   **tablespoon unsalted butter**

INSTRUCTIONS:

1. Adjust oven rack to middle position and heat oven to 350 degrees. Line rimmed baking sheet with parchment paper and spread nuts in even layer. Toast 4 minutes, rotate pan, and continue toasting until fragrant, about 4 minutes. Transfer baking sheet to wire rack.

2. Stir together ingredients for spice mix in medium bowl and set aside.

3. Bring rum, vanilla, sugar, and butter to a boil in medium saucepan, whisking constantly. Stir in toasted nuts and cook, stirring constantly with wooden spoon, until nuts are shiny and almost all liquid has evaporated, about 1½ minutes. Transfer nuts to bowl with spice mix and toss to coat well. Return nuts to parchment-lined baking sheet to cool.

⠿ VARIATION:

Mexican-Spiced Almonds, Peanuts, and Pumpkin Seeds

Following recipe for Warm-Spiced Pecans with Rum Glaze, replace pecans with 1¼ cups sliced almonds, ⅔ cup roasted unsalted peanuts, and ¼ cup raw pumpkin seeds. Toast almonds for 4 minutes, then add peanuts and pumpkin seeds to baking sheet and toast 4 minutes longer.

Replace Warm Spice Mix with 1 tablespoon sugar, 1 teaspoon kosher salt, ¼ teaspoon ground cinnamon, ¼ teaspoon ground cumin, ¼ teaspoon ground coriander, ⅛ teaspoon cayenne, and ⅛ teaspoon garlic powder. Replace rum and vanilla with 2 tablespoons water.

i n d e x